Whispers of Encouragement

Every Day Inspiration for Women

Inspired by Faith

Whispers of Encouragement

Whispers of Encouragement

ISBN 978-0-9859685-3-3

Published by Product Concept Mfg., Inc.
2175 N. Academy Circle #200, Colorado Springs, CO 80909

Written and Compiled by Patricia Mitchell
in association with Product Concept Mfg., Inc.

All scripture quotations are from the King James version of the Bible unless otherwise noted.

Sayings not having a credit listed are contributed by writers for Product Concept Mfg., Inc. or in a rare case, the author is unknown.

Whispers of Encouragement

Though our feelings come and go,
God's love for us does not.

C.S. Lewis

Whispers of Encouragement is a book of reflections and time-honored quotations designed to inspire you, guide you, and lift up your heart. Each reflection explores a theme that touches your life, such as knowing what you really want...finding peace of heart and mind...enriching your relationship with others and with God.

We invite you to use this book as a daily devotional, or as your source whenever you need an emotional boost...a spiritual pick-me-up...or simply a good word. It's our prayer that *Whispers* will bless you with hope and encouragement as you move forward today in faith, love, and confidence.

Purpose

Purpose is what gives life a meaning.

Charles H. Parkhurst

DISCOVERING LIFE'S PURPOSE

In the beginning years of life, our purpose isn't something we think about. We're too busy growing and learning, making friends and discovering the world. As we grow older, however, we often start wondering what lifes is all about. Sometimes what used to motivate us doesn't anymore. The things we were passionate about in the past have lost their power to excite.

If you know the feeling, take heart. Your life still has purpose, but it may have changed from what it was in the past. You have more experience, more insight, and more wisdom than you did, say, 10 or 20 years ago. Doesn't it make sense that God might have something new for you to do–something that uses today's circumstances, interests, and opportunities?

Discover (or reaffirm) your life's purpose by thinking about what really means the most to you right now. Then ask yourself whether what you're actually doing right now supports your priorities and values, or is likely to take you where you want to go. Most importantly, let God weigh in on the subject. Open yourself to His guidance, His prompting, His purpose. Without a doubt, He has a beautiful one for you–enjoy!

Do all to the glory of God.
1 Corinthians 10:31

Have a purpose in life, and, having it, throw such strength of mind and muscle into your work as God has given you.
Thomas Carlyle

Great minds have purposes; others have wishes.
Washington Irving

The object of all work is production or accomplishment, and to either of these ends there must be forethought, system, planning, intelligence, and honest purpose, as well as perspiration. Seeming to do is not doing.
Thomas Alva Edison

If God can work through me,
he can work through anyone.
FRANCIS OF ASSISI

What do you want most to do?
That's what I have to keep asking myself,
in the face of difficulties.
KATHERINE MANSFIELD

This is the true joy in life,
being used for a purpose recognized
by yourself as a mighty one.
GEORGE BERNARD SHAW

In a world where there is so much
to be done, I felt strongly impressed
that there must be something
for me to do.
DOROTHEA DIX

Renewal

He restores my soul.

Psalm 23:3 NIV

Renewal Time

"A woman's work is never done," the old adage says...and let's add our hearty "Amen!" Our work and responsibilities carry us from dawn to dusk, and all too often, far into the night. A day off? You're kidding, right?

Every to-do we have on our list today stands in the way of rest and renewal, yet only rest and renewal can keep us going, doing the things we need to do and want to do. So perhaps it's high time we define "relaxation" not as a luxury for imaginary women of endless leisure, but a vital necessity for each one of us.

How you rest, renew, and restore yourself physically and emotionally is up to you. Maybe a brisk walk does the trick...or a 20-minute nap...or time spent in prayer and meditation... or a stint at the piano or sewing machine. What's important isn't so much what you do, but that it works for you, and you do it for you.

Look at it this way: If a woman's work is never done, a little time out won't make a whole lot of difference, will it? But it will make a big, big difference to you!

Within you there is a stillness
and a sanctuary to which you can retreat
at any time and be yourself.
HERMANN HESSE

It's only by forgetting yourself
that you draw near to God.
HENRY DAVID THOREAU

Every now and then go away,
have a little relaxation, for when you come back
to your work, your judgment will be surer.
LEONARDO DA VINCI

Take rest; a field that has rested
gives a bountiful crop.
OVID

We must always change, renew,
rejuvenate ourselves; otherwise we harden.
JOHANN WOLFGANG VON GOETHE

True silence is the rest of the mind;
it is to the spirit what sleep is to the body,
nourishment and refreshment.
WILLIAM PENN

He enjoys true leisure who has time
to improve his soul's estate.
HENRY DAVID THOREAU

What I dream of is an art of balance, of purity
and serenity devoid of troubling or depressing
subject matter–a soothing, calming influence
on the mind, rather like a good armchair which
provides relaxation from physical fatigue.
HENRI MATISSE

Opportunity

Knock, and it shall be opened unto you.

Matthew 7:7

THE DOOR OF OPPORTUNITY

If we think we've never missed an opportunity, then we've been walking around with our eyes closed! Yes, many an opportunity has passed us by because we weren't expecting it...we didn't recognize it...we had other priorities...we were afraid to grab it and run with it.

If you think about a few of your missed opportunities, you'll gain a good insight into your values, expectations, emotions, and perspective. Some opportunities you purposely passed up because they didn't fit with your goals (good for you!), but others you may have failed to grasp because you were fearful, undecided, or over-cautious. So next time, what will you do? Use these missed opportunities as an opportunity to learn about yourself and grow where you need to.

God invites you to ask Him for the opportunities you desire. Then, open your eyes to the opportunities He sends. Sometimes a great opportunity is like a wide-open door, and all you need to do is put one foot in front of the other and walk through it. Other times, a fantastic opportunity lies hidden behind a door you need to push open with effort...imagination... faith in yourself and your abilities.

However God sends it, opportunity is yours.

The world is all gates, all opportunities, strings of tension waiting to be struck.

Ralph Waldo Emerson

I was seldom able to see an opportunity until it had ceased to be one.

Mark Twain

The great opportunity is where you are. Do not despise your own place and hour. Every place is under the stars, every place is the center of the world.

John Burroughs

To improve the golden moment of opportunity, and catch the good that is within our reach, is the great art of life.

Samuel Johnson

To succeed, jump as quickly at opportunities as you do at conclusions.

Benjamin Franklin

You had better live your best and act your best and think your best today; for today is the sure preparation for tomorrow and all the other tomorrows that follow.

Harriet Martineau

Opportunity is missed by most people because it is dressed in overalls and looks like work.

Thomas Alva Edison

The opportunity that God sends does not wake up him who is asleep.

Proverb

Forgive

The heart has always the pardoning power.

Anne-Sophie Swetchine

THE POWER OF FORGIVENESS

Forgiveness begins in the heart. Why? Because that's where old animosities simmer and new hurts fester with every real or imagined offense. Often even sincere apologies and earnest reconciliations fail to heal the sore inside, and the bitter memory of what happened lingers for a lifetime.

Failure to forgive is a heavy burden, and it's humanly impossible to shake it off. Releasing yourself from its grip requires strength that doesn't come naturally to anyone. God's Spirit at work in your heart, however, provides all the power you need. Here's how: First, He opens His arms to you in complete forgiveness, erasing your guilt and setting an example of forgiveness for you to follow. Second, He invites you to remember that others have weaknesses, too. Shouldn't they receive the same measure of compassion that you receive from God? Of course.

Third, your heavenly Father showers the forgiven and forgiving heart with peace, gentleness, and spiritual wisdom, the wisdom that allows us to accept ourselves and others as we really are—weak, bumbling around at this adventure called life; frequently misguided and wrong, but at the same time, beloved sons and daughters of God.

Forgive us our debts, as we forgive our debtors.
MATTHEW 6:12

Forgiveness saves the expense of anger,
the cost of hatred.
HANNAH MORE

When Christ says, "Forgive your enemies,"
it is not for the sake of the enemy,
but for one's own sake that he says so.
OSCAR WILDE

Better by far you should forget and smile,
than that you should remember and be sad.
CHRISTINA ROSSETTI

Life appears to me too short to be spent in nursing animosity or registering wrong.

CHARLOTTE BRONTË

The man who cannot forgive any mortal thing is a green hand in life.

ROBERT LOUIS STEVENSON

When you go to bed at night, have for your pillow three things–love, hope and forgiveness. And you will awaken in the morning with a song in your heart.

VICTOR HUGO

It is in pardoning that we are pardoned.

FRANCIS OF ASSISI

Laugh

He that is of a merry heart hath a continual feast.

Proverbs 15:15

Plenty of Laughter

What's there to laugh at? Plenty! Trouble is, we get so caught up in our own problems, others' problems, and the world's problems that we think the only thing there's plenty of is problems.

Well, there are plenty of problems, and maybe that's the best reason of all to look for plenty of laughs.

If you can crack a smile at a baby's toothless grin...get tickled to remember an uncle's corny jokes...chuckle at the cartoon-a-day you've subscribed to...giggle with your girlfriends at nothing in particular...savor the silliness of your favorite sitcom...laugh out loud at your own slip-ups and stumbles, you'll always have plenty of laughter in your life.

And laughter is serious stuff. It relieves tension, relaxes the mind, and brings problems (plenty of them) down to manageable size. It's a God-given gift that comes easily to some of us. Others of us have to work at it, but it's well worth the effort. Laughter starts with a smile and goes on from there. It's learnable, doable, and most of all, fun.

(Look for signs that God has a sense of humor, too–just spend some time watching the creatures and critters He created!)

We are all here for a spell;
get all the good laughs you can.
WILL ROGERS

Laughter is the sun that drives
winter from the human face.
VICTOR HUGO

Mirth is God's medicine.
Everybody ought to bathe in it.
HENRY WARD BEECHER

Laughter is the sensation of feeling good all over
and showing it principally in one place.
JOSH BILLINGS

One should take good care not to grow too wise
for so great a pleasure of life as laughter.

Joseph Addison

Laughter has something in it common with the
ancient words of faith and inspiration;
it unfreezes pride and unwinds secrecy;
it makes men forget themselves in the presence
of something greater than themselves.

G. K. Chesterton

Honest good humor is the oil and wine of a
merry meeting, and there is no jovial
companionship equal to that where the jokes are
rather small and the laughter abundant.

Washington Irving

Peace

Peace I leave with you.

John 14:27

THE POSSIBILITY OF PEACE

Peace! Is it possible in a world of ornery people and contentious arguments? Is it thinkable when there's so much turbulence and turmoil swirling around us? Without a doubt, if we wait for peace to break out between all people and every nation before we're at peace, we'll be waiting a long, long time! Yet real peace–genuine peace–doesn't come from the outside, but from within the heart.

Inner peace begins not with other people, but with your own strong, healthy, and positive relationship with God. His Spirit at work in you builds this kind of relationship as you allow Him to guide your choices and decisions. His peace grows as you trust His willingness to forgive whatever you bring to Him, and let love for Him fill your heart and mind.

God's peace provides a place of shelter and serenity no further away than your own heart and soul. Despite the challenging behavior of others or hectic events of the day, you remain at peace–a deep stillness that others perceive in your actions, hear in your voice, and feel in the way you touch them with peace.

Yes, chaos is catching–but so is peace.

Never be in a hurry; do everything quietly and in a calm spirit. Do not lose your inner peace for anything whatsoever, even if your whole world seems upset.

FRANCIS DE SALES

In struggling against anguish one never produces serenity; the struggle against anguish only produces new forms of anguish.

SIMONE WEIL

He who lives in harmony with himself lives in harmony with the universe.

MARCUS AURELIUS

First keep the peace within yourself,
then you can also bring peace to others.

THOMAS À KEMPIS

We must learn an inner solitude wherever or with whomsoever we may be. We must learn to penetrate things and find God there.

MEISTER ECKHART

God cannot give us a happiness and peace apart from Himself, because it is not there. There is no such thing.

C. S. LEWIS

Pray

Pray without ceasing.

1 Thessalonians 5:17

The Prayer Connection

It would be hard to imagine a good relationship without communication. There's a natural desire to connect with the people we love by speaking to them face to face, or by reaching out to them via the various electronic gadgets available to us.

God loves you and wants a relationship with you, and so He desires to communicate with you. You hear His message in the words of Scripture, and He longs to hear your voice in prayer. See, prayer is you in communication with God!

Perhaps you prefer praying aloud among many gathered together, or whispering your words in the privacy of your heart. Either way, God hears. Perhaps you like reciting your prayers in time-honored phrases, or speaking them spontaneously in the language of everyday. Either way, God listens. Long or short, formal or casual, prayer is your ongoing conversation with God.

Prayer is profound, yet simple. Prayer expresses gratitude to the One who created you, the world and everything in it. It extends a heartfelt request to the One who comforts, forgives, strengthens, and assists you. Prayer sounds a song of thanksgiving to the One who richly blesses you.

In your good relationship with God, there's communication. There's prayer.

In every thing by prayer and supplication with thanksgiving let your requests be made known unto God.

PHILIPPIANS 4:6

Prayer is not eloquence, but earnestness; not the definition of helplessness, but the feeling of it; not figures of speech, but compunction of soul.

HANNAH MORE

There is not in the world a kind of life more sweet and delightful than that of a continual conversation with God.

BROTHER LAWRENCE

There are moments when, whatever be the attitude of the body, the soul is on its knees.

VICTOR HUGO

Prayer is not overcoming God's reluctance,
but laying hold of His willingness.
MARTIN LUTHER

Prayer should be the key of the day
and the lock of the night.
PROVERB

Nothing is too small a subject for prayer,
because nothing is too small
to be the subject of God's care.
HENRY THOMAS HAMBLIN

Direct all your prayers to one thing only, that is,
to conform your will perfectly to the Divine will.
TERESA OF AVILA

Courage

Be of good courage.

Psalm 31:24

Courage To Try

When it gets dark outside, do something you probably haven't done since you were a child: look out the window and wish upon a star. What is the wish that will float from your heart into the shadowed nighttime skies? Perhaps it has to do with yourself or someone you care about.

Perhaps it's a dream that's been in the back of your mind for years, or something you've told yourself you'll do...someday.

The twinkling star, of course, has no power to grant your wish, but you do. There's a step you can take now toward a distant dream, a start you can make to a long-term project, a beginning you can initiate today to get you where you want to be tomorrow.

More important than any wish is what you do about it. Do nothing, and there's no use wishing. Wish, but then do something. Even if you don't manage to get everything you're wishing for, you've done what mere wishing can never do, and that's show courage–courage to step out. Courage to try.

Every time you look up at the sky, look up at the stars–and shine along with the best of them!

Courage is the greatest of all the virtues, because if you haven't courage, you may not have an opportunity to use any of the others.

Samuel Johnson

It is not because things are difficult that we do not dare; it is because we do not dare that they are difficult.

Seneca

If you limit your actions in life to things that nobody can possibly find fault with, you will not do much.

Lewis Carroll

Courage is resistance to fear, mastery of fear, not absence of fear.

Mark Twain

Providence has hidden a charm in difficult undertakings, which is appreciated only by those who dare to grapple with them.

Anne-Sophie Swetchine

Be strong in the Lord,
and in the power of His might.

Ephesians 6:10

Courage is not simply one of the virtues, but the form of every virtue at the testing point.

C. S. Lewis

For of all sad words of tongue or pen,
The saddest are these: It might have been.

John Greenleaf Whittier

Simplicity

Nothing is better than simplicity.

Walt Whitman

THE BEAUTY OF SIMPLICITY

Ah, the simple life! A lakeside cabin...afternoons in the hammock...few wants, few needs. For most of us, though, that kind of simple life lasts no longer than a summer vacation. Real life hands us a lengthy list of responsibilities, makes multiple demands on our time, and includes an ever-increasing number of wants and needs.

Yet real-life simple life is possible. This kind of simple life counters many popular notions, but sometimes going against the flow is a good thing. Consider these ideas:

- Focus on activities that matter to you. If it's not essential, doesn't enhance your life, and doesn't interest you, don't do it. The simple life means you're comfortable saying a simple word, and that word is, No.
- Think before you buy. If it's not necessary, won't add enjoyment or beauty to your life, or costs more than you can afford, let it go. Why give yourself something else to dust, wash, repair, and clean? Again, that simple word.
- Indulge in simple pleasures. Sip a cup of hot chocolate. Curl up with a good book. Pet a cat. Walk a dog. Yes!

God has given you everything you need for a simply beautiful life.

I have lived long enough to learn how much there is I can really do without.

Socrates

I am bound to praise the simple life, because I have lived it and found it good.

John Burroughs

You don't need nine-tenths of the things you scramble for. Don't be afraid to have nothing. Happiness is not what you have, but who you are. You are already who you need to be.

Diogenes

Simplicity in character, in manners, in style,
in all things, the supreme excellence is simplicity.

HENRY WADSWORTH LONGFELLOW

The best things are nearest: breath in your nostrils, light in your eyes, flowers at your feet, duties at your hand, the path of right just before you. Then do not grasp at the stars, but do life's plain, common work as it comes, certain that daily duties and daily bread are the sweetest things of life.

ROBERT LOUIS STEVENSON

Simplicity, simplicity, simplicity!
I say let your affairs be as two, three,
and not a hundred or a thousand.

HENRY DAVID THOREAU

Gratitude

In every thing give thanks.

1 Thessalonians 5:18

Words of Thanks

What do you feel good about right now? Perhaps an avalanche of words and pictures are flowing from your heart...or maybe not. Perhaps there's only a trickle of things you can honestly say you feel good about. In either case, give thanks!

What do you wish were better right now? Again, maybe an avalanche...maybe a trickle...of things you would like to change, or make go away completely. In either case, give thanks!

Gratitude opens each day with thanksgiving for the gifts of life and breath, thoughts and feelings, abilities and experiences. From the perspective of genuine gratitude, there's no difference between what we find enjoyable and what we don't. Though one brings temporary pleasure, the other brings knowledge, maturity, and insight.

Sure, it's hard to thank God when things are going wrong. But even in heartbreaking situations, we can thank Him for the friend who is there for us...the physician who guides us through treatment...the difficult truths uncovered and dealt with so emotional healing can begin.

Even if you can think of only one or two things you're truly thankful for right now, give thanks for them. Let your words lead you to many more reasons for genuine, heartfelt gratitude.

Give thanks unto the LORD;
for he is good: for his mercy endureth for ever.
PSALM 106:1

A thankful heart is not only the greatest virtue,
but the parent of all other virtues.
CICERO

When you arise in the morning, think of what
a precious privilege it is to be alive–
to breathe, to think, to enjoy, to love.
MARCUS AURELIUS

The person who has stopped being thankful has
fallen asleep in life.
ROBERT LOUIS STEVENSON

If any one would tell you the shortest,
surest way to all happiness, and all perfection,
he must tell you to make it a rule to your self, to
thank and praise God for every thing
that happens to you. For it is certain,
that whatever seeming calamity happens to you,
if you thank and praise God for it,
you turn it into a blessing.

WILLIAM LAW

We must give ourselves more earnestly and
intelligently and generously than we have to the
happy duty of appreciation.

MARIANA GRISWOLD VAN RENSSELAER

Let the thankful heart sweep through the day
and, as the magnet finds the iron, so it will find,
in every hour, some heavenly blessings!

HENRY WARD BEECHER

Kindness

Be ye kind one to another.

Ephesians 4:32

The Gift of Kindness

We learn by example. Perhaps that's why God continues to show us kindness after kindness. "This is what I mean!" we can imagine Him saying as He grants us another new day, even though we've made a mess of the last one. "Here's how!" God explains as He assures us of His forgiveness and understanding, despite the fact we haven't been a paragon of perfection lately.

With God's Spirit at work in our hearts (another kindness!), we have what it takes to extend God-style kindness to others. We can meet harshness with gentleness...coldness with warmth...offense with understanding. We can show compassion, even when others don't seem to notice or care, just like God.

And just as God's unfailing kindness might surprise you, your constant kindness to others is sure to get some startled looks. Nowadays, who stops to hold the door open for a mom struggling with two toddlers and a stroller? Who even notices the wheelchair-bound shopper straining to reach a can of tomatoes on the top shelf? Who takes time to listen while a lonely neighbor rambles on about his medical condition for the umpteenth time?

Who does? You do, because God has shown you how.

Have you had a kindness shown?

Pass it on;

'Twas not given for thee alone,

Pass it on;

Let it travel down the years,

Let it wipe another's tears,

Till in Heaven the deed appears–

Pass it on.

HENRY BURTON

I expect to pass through this world but once. Any good therefore that I can do, or any kindness I can show to any fellow creature, let me do it now. Let me not defer or neglect it, for I shall not pass this way again.

William Penn

To cultivate kindness is a valuable part of the business of life.

Samuel Johnson

Kindness is the language which the deaf can hear and the blind can see.

Mark Twain

Three things in human life are important. The first is to be kind. The second is to be kind. And the third is to be kind.

Henry James

Patience

Love is patient.

1 Corinthians 13:4 NIV

Sweet Patience

When we're hurting, healing can't come soon enough. When we're overwhelmed by questions, it's not easy to wait for answers. We want healing, we want answers, now! Yet in our impatience to heal, either physically or emotionally, we often deny the extent of our injury. In our impatience to get answers, we're apt to accept ineffective solutions or simple–but wrong– explanations.

The body's time...the heart's time...God's time...is not the same as our time. Just as a planted seed must wait for warming rains before it grows and flowers bloom, so we are obliged to pause...sometimes to stop...and wait. Wait for the right time, the right place, for true healing to begin...for truthful and satisfying answers to come our way.

Even minor things, like a long line at the grocery store or a traffic jam on the highway, start our fingers drumming in annoyance. But perhaps we could use some of those minor things to begin practicing a major thing: the art of patience. We could smile instead of scowl. We could relax instead of honk.

"Patience is a bitter plant," an old saying goes, "but its fruit is always sweet."

Patience is the companion of wisdom.

AUGUSTINE

*Experience has taught me this,
that we undo ourselves by impatience.
Misfortunes have their life and their limits,
their sickness and their health.*

MICHEL DE MONTAIGNE

*Only those who have the patience to do
simple things perfectly will acquire the skill to
do difficult things easily.*

JOHANN VON SCHILLER

*Patience and diligence, like faith,
remove mountains.*

WILLIAM PENN

Have patience with all things,
but first of all with yourself.
Francis de Sales

Patience serves as a protection against wrongs as clothes do against cold. For if you put on more clothes as the cold increases, it will have no power to hurt you. So in like manner, you must grow in patience when you meet with great wrongs, and they will then be powerless to vex your mind.
Leonardo da Vinci

Wait on the LORD.
Psalm 27:14

Patience strengthens the spirit, sweetens the temper, stifles anger, extinguishes envy, subdues pride, bridles the tongue, restrains the hand, and tramples upon temptations.
George Horne

Love

God is love.

1 John 4:8

Living Love

"I love you." How easily those three little words trip off the tongue! And it's important to say them often, because they bring comfort, assurance, and warmth to those who mean the most to us. Yet unless loving acts follow, "I love you" is nothing more than three little words.

Loving acts don't need to be big or spectacular. They're not loud or showy. Arguably, the most meaningful acts of love rest in little things, like a word of encouragement, a relaxed and friendly chat, a whispered endearment. And love doesn't always use words, as when we put others ahead of ourselves, show courtesy and goodwill, and assist those who need our help.

God's love, too, is more than just words–much, much more. He invites you to pray to Him and promises to listen. He yearns for you to sense His presence, to feel His pleasure in you, and to experience His peace. Your God delights to enfold you in the warmth and security of His living and active love.

Love-in-action cares and nurtures, protects and cherishes. It gives freely and cheerfully. Though love is spoken with the lips, it is a matter of the heart.

We have too many high-sounding words and too few actions that correspond with them.

Abigail Adams

Faces are but a gallery of pictures, and talk but a tinkling cymbal, where there is no love.

Francis Bacon

To love anyone is nothing else than to wish that person good.

Thomas Aquinas

Instead of allowing yourself to be unhappy, just let your love grow as God wants it to grow. Seek goodness in others. Love more persons more. Love them more impersonally, more unselfishly, without thought of return. The return, never fear, will take care of itself.

Henry Drummond

Love is never lost. If not reciprocated, it will flow back and soften and purify the heart.

Washington Irving

True love demands nothing, seeks nothing for its own, but desires only to give. If we love God and our neighbor, we desire only to give, to serve, to pour out all that we have at the feet of Life.

Henry Thomas Hamblin

Happiness

If you want to be
happy, be.

Leo Tolstoy

A Happy Face

Do you want in on a beauty secret? It doesn't come in a tiny glass jar, and it won't cost you a small fortune, either. What's more, you can wear as much as you want all day, every day, and it remains as fresh as the moment you put it on. The secret? Happiness.

Here's a two-step way to discover the secret for yourself. Step one: Look in a mirror and crinkle your forehead so worry lines show. Frown. Do your best impression of a very angry woman. Now stop! (You wouldn't want it to freeze that way!) Proceed to step two: Smile. Think of something that makes you feel good inside. See the difference? Make-up or no make-up, you look beautiful!

Yes, you may say, but sometimes I don't feel happy. So what? Happy women aren't those without problems, but those who are happy despite their problems. They aren't about to let some silly old problems stand in the way of their favorite beautifier!

Another secret: When you choose happiness over sadness...a smile over a frown...joy over misery, you'll not only look better to the world, but the world will look better to you.

The grand essentials to happiness in this life are something to do, something to love, and something to hope for.

Joseph Addison

Fear less, hope more; eat less, chew more; whine less, breathe more; talk less, say more; love more, and all good things will be yours.

Proverb

The happiness of life is made up of minute fractions—the little, soon-forgotten charities of a kiss or smile, a kind look, a heartfelt compliment, and the countless infinitesimals of pleasurable and genial feeling.

Samuel Coleridge

In simple pathways hand in hand with duty
(With faith and love, too, ever at her side),
May happiness be met in all her beauty
The while we search for her both far and wide.
Seeking for happiness we find the way
Doing the things we ought to do each day.

Ella Wheeler Wilcox

Serenity

Cast all your anxiety on him.

1 Peter 5:7 NIV

REST AT EASE

Agreed: Worry is useless. But we worry anyway! And there's no end of things to worry about, is there? Health. Finances. Politics. Relationships. Today. The future. Scary "what ifs...?"

haunt our thoughts, and we lose sleep imagining all the worst-case scenarios that could possibly take place.

Now how about another kind of "what if...?" What if you put today and every day in God's hands? What if you admit to Him that you have no idea what the future holds, but you trust His wisdom and judgment? What if you toss all your worries into a great big box, seal it tight, and push the whole thing over to Him? What if?

Why not? God invites you to bring your burdens to Him and leave them with Him. He encourages you to rest at ease, because He will never leave you, no matter what happens. You have Him to call on for help and strength, and you can hold onto Him whenever you feel things are getting out of control.

When it comes to God's desire to take away your worries, there's no "what if" about it. He will do it.

The sovereign cure for worry is prayer.
William James

Worry is an infirmity; there is no virtue in it.
Worry is spiritual nearsightedness;
a fumbling way of looking at little things
and of magnifying their value.
Anna Brown Lindsay

Worry is interest paid on trouble
before it falls due.
W R Inge

Nothing is so wretched or foolish as to anticipate
misfortunes. What madness is it to be expecting
evil before it comes.
Seneca

I am an old man and have known
a great many troubles, but most of them
have never happened.

MARK TWAIN

Do you wish to live in tension? By no means. No one who is in a state of fear or sorrow or tension is free, but whoever is delivered from sorrows or fears or anxieties, he is at the same time delivered from servitude.

EPICTETUS

Take therefore no thought for the morrow:
for the morrow shall take thought
for the things of itself.

MATTHEW 6:34

Contentment

*Be content with
what you have.*

Hebrews 13:5 NIV

Completely Content

Complete contentment with who we are and what we have...genuine satisfaction with our place in the world...is it possible? And is it even desirable in a world where we're expected to strive, achieve, and attain? The answer to both questions is Yes.

Yes, not simply to possibility, but to certainty that heart-deep satisfaction is yours when you know you're a beloved child of God. You were born in a certain place and at a certain time according to God's plan. There's a reason you are who you are and where you are right now. Contentment comes from knowing you have everything you need in Him.

Yes, not simply to going forward, but to God-pleasing growth and spiritual maturity. God has provided you with resources He expects you to use for your benefit and for the benefit of others. He sends opportunities He invites you to take, and He has given you talents, skills, and abilities to enhance your life and the lives of those around you. Contentment comes from believing that a fulfilling life is one of progressive change for the better.

Contentment is a choice you make every day.

The greater part of our happiness or misery
depends upon our dispositions,
and not upon our circumstances.
Martha Washington

I have learned, in whatsoever state I am,
therewith to be content.
Philippians 4:11

A contented mind is the greatest blessing a man
can enjoy in this world.
Joseph Addison

Learn to be pleased with everything; with
wealth, so far as it made us beneficial to others;
with power, for not having much to care for;
and with obscurity, for being unenvied.
Plutarch

Godliness with contentment is great gain.
1 TIMOTHY 6:6

Contentment makes poor men rich;
discontentment makes rich men poor.
BENJAMIN FRANKLIN

The best of blessings—a contented mind.
PROVERB

When we cannot find contentment in ourselves,
it is useless to seek it elsewhere.
FRANÇOIS DE LA ROCHEFOUCAULD

Comfort

Adversity is the first path to truth.

George Gordon Byron

Comfort In Adversity

"God's in His heaven," the poet Robert Browning wrote. "All's right with the world!" Those words express our feelings exactly when everything's going our way. God's in His heaven smoothing the path ahead, opening doors of opportunity, and blessing us with more than we ever imagined. All's right with the world!

But things change. Big plans fall through, cherished hopes vanish, and what we've worked so hard to achieve comes to nothing. Suddenly at a standstill, we wonder if God has tumbled out of His place in the sky...if He no longer cares what happens to us...if we did something to anger Him, because nothing's right with our world.

Though it's hard to believe, times like these are blessings. To comfort you, God comes down from His heaven to walk with you, teaching you to rely on Him as He leads you safely through challenges, hardships, and problems. Without the blessing of difficult times, you would never have a chance to experience the depth of His care for you in all circumstances.

In difficult times, as in wonderful times, God is in His heaven...and on His Earth...and all's right with you...all's right with the world.

*You have trusted Him in a few things,
and He has not failed you. Trust Him now for
everything, and see if He does not do for you
exceeding abundantly above all that you
could ever have asked or even thought.*

Hannah Whitall Smith

*There's a tremendous amount to be gained
through what appears to be adversity.
If we don't allow the crisis, these challenges
to take place, then we remain fixed in life
and never really ripen or mature.*

Thomas More

Were you to simply remain in God's presence, that would be a great help to you, supporting you in your troubles and helping you to bear them patiently. Be sure that God is more ready than ever to welcome you into his arms, and that as your distress increases, so does his mercy towards you increase and abound.

John-Baptiste de La Salle

Misfortune is never mournful to the soul that accepts it; for such do always see that in every cloud is an angel's face.

St. Jerome

Man meets with adversity and fights it tooth and nail, as something evil, not knowing that it is merely a preparation for greater things and a larger and fuller life.

Henry Thomas Hamblin

Joy

Scatter joy!

Ralph Waldo Emerson

HEART-DEEP JOY

Are you a joyful person? If you think you're not, maybe it's because you don't go around with a permanent grin fixed on your face. After all, some days there's not much to grin about!

Or maybe you're the kind of person who doesn't try to hide from or deny the less-than-joyful aspects of life. Some things are bad news, pure and simple.

True joy goes much deeper than how you feel about what's going on at the moment. Joy is like a steady, inner light that keeps you resilient, upbeat, and optimistic through all the ups and downs of your day. It's a shield against being overcome by despair or stymied by discouragement. It puts the brakes on negative thinking and harmful emotions that rob life of joy.

Real, honest-to-goodness joy is a gift of God, and one He freely gives. His gift of joy stems from the willingness to let go of fear, express gratitude for life's blessings, and find satisfaction in serving others. As a joyful person, you rely on God's strength, His wisdom, and His unconditional love for you. Though you might not always wear an ear-to-ear smile, the light in your eyes, the gentleness of your words, and the confidence in your step will ever radiate heart-to-heart joy.

All who joy would win must share it;
happiness was born a twin.
GEORGE GORDON BYRON

My soul shall be joyful in the LORD.
PSALM 35:9

Real joy comes not from ease or riches
or from the praise of men,
but from doing something worthwhile.
WILFRED GRENFELL

Let us be grateful to people who make us happy;
they are the charming gardeners
who make our souls blossom.

MARCEL PROUST

Joy is not in things; it is in us.

RICHARD WAGNER

Happiness is as a butterfly which,
when pursued, is always beyond our grasp,
but which if you will sit down quietly,
may alight upon you.

NATHANIEL HAWTHORNE

Find ecstasy in life;
the mere sense of living is joy enough.

EMILY DICKINSON

Change

God alone is changeless.

Teresa of Avila

THREE A'S FOR CHANGE

Just as summer turns to winter, change can darken our days and hide the sunlight we had so long enjoyed. And just as winter yields to spring, change can chase away shadows, generate life, and open our eyes to new horizons. Change is not always welcome, but change is life itself.

So how about these three A's for handling change?

- Accept change, because to do otherwise sinks your mood and saps your energy. What has happened has happened, and you can't undo it.
- Adapt to the new situation. Remain flexible and teachable so you won't miss opportunities that this change may have brought to you.
- Act with goodwill and optimism. Find the most positive and productive way of responding, no matter how you feel. (Your positive actions and attitude will soon dispel, or at least diminish, negative feelings.)

And remember, you're walking with God, who never changes. His love for you is the same, no matter what life brings your way. His care for you remains constant, and His commitment to you is as strong and steady as ever. Here's another A: Allow your changeless God to use the change in your life to bring you closer to Him.

Wherever we are, it is but a stage on the way to somewhere else, and whatever we do, however well we do it, it is only a preparation to do something else that shall be different.

ROBERT LOUIS STEVENSON

The old woman I shall become will be quite different from the woman I am now. Another I is beginning.

GEORGE SAND

Today is not yesterday: we ourselves change; how can our works and thoughts, if they are always to be the fittest, continue always the same? Change, indeed is painful; yet ever needful.

THOMAS CARLYLE

We know that all things work together for good to them that love God.

ROMANS 8:28

Life belongs to the living,
and he who lives must be prepared for changes.
Johann Wolfgang von Goethe

When people shake their heads
because we are living in a restless age,
ask them how they would like to live in
a stationary one and do without change.
George Bernard Shaw

To every thing there is a season,
and a time to every purpose under the heaven.
Ecclesiastes 3:1

Keep the currents moving.
Don't let your life stagnate.
John Burroughs

Compliments

*Well done, good
and faithful servant.*

Matthew 25:23

Compliments to You

Well-deserved compliments often fail to materialize. Someone may have meant to tell you what a good job you did, but forgot to say it. Or maybe they planned to send a thank-you note, but got distracted by something else.

So there's nothing wrong–and everything right–about handing out a few good words to yourself. For every job well done, congratulate yourself. Give yourself a pat on the back when you do a favor for someone, go out of your way to help, or bite your tongue rather than make a snarky comment. Smile when you look in the mirror and see yourself–the very woman who's managing a household, caring for her loved ones, cherishing her friends, and using her skills and talents in her church and community.

Celebrate the gifts God has given to you and respect them by using them in positive, productive, and compliment-worthy ways. Give Him the glory for all you're able to do, because you have been blessed. Feel good about yourself, because God feels good about you.

And when the compliments come from others, put a smile on your face. Graciously thank them for their thoughtful words, and smile inside, too, because you know you've earned them!

It is difficult to make a man miserable while he feels he is worthy of himself and claims kindred to the great God who made him.

ABRAHAM LINCOLN

Friendship with one's self is all important, because without it one cannot be friends with anyone else in the world.

ELEANOR ROOSEVELT

He who undervalues himself is justly undervalued by others.

WILLIAM HAZLITT

A man cannot be comfortable
without his own approval.
MARK TWAIN

I care not so much what I am to others
as what I am to myself. I will be rich by myself,
and not by borrowing.
MICHEL DE MONTAIGNE

That kind of life is most happy
which affords us most opportunities
of gaining our own esteem.
SAMUEL JOHNSON

Miracles

Life itself is the
miracle of miracles.

George Bernard Shaw

SEEING THE MIRACLES

Many of us claim that we live a pretty ordinary life. We cherish our loved ones and see to our daily responsibilities. We're unsurprised to see flowers blooming, hear birds chirping, and to be able to soak up rays of buttery sunshine. We expect to breathe, feel, think, laugh, imagine, and dream today.

But aren't all these things miracles–your friends and family, yourself, everything you do, and all creation? Yes! These are God's "ordinary" miracles, the ones we're apt to take for granted, because–miracle of miracles!–they take place day after day, month after month, season after season. Each is by itself extraordinary (think about it!), and together they create a mosaic of marvelous things for us to see, savor, and enjoy.

At times, God chooses to intervene with a miraculous healing, an incredible coincidence, an inexplicable turn of events. These are miracles most visible–and perhaps only visible–to eyes focused on His wondrous work day in and day out in all creation.

Truly, God has put you in a world of miracles. Why not take a few moments to list a few of them? Then give thanks for each one! Do the same every day, because every day is full of miracles, great and small.

The man who does not believe
in miracles surely makes it certain that
he will never take part in one.

WILLIAM BLAKE

All change is a miracle to contemplate; but it is
a miracle which is taking place every second.

HENRY DAVID THOREAU

This is the LORD's doing;
it is marvellous in our eyes.

PSALM 118:23

The invariable mark of wisdom is to see the
miraculous in the common.

RALPH WALDO EMERSON

A gentle word, a kind look,
a good-natured smile can work wonders
and accomplish miracles.
William Hazlitt

The most incredible thing
about miracles is that they happen.
G. K. Chesterton

Seeing, hearing, feeling, are miracles,
and each part and tag of me is a miracle.
Walt Whitman

Where there is great love,
there are always miracles.
Willa Cather

Habits

As the snowflakes gather,
so our habits are formed.

Thomas Bentham

THOUGHT-FULL HABITS

Most of us can name at least one habit we wish we didn't have. Often we've tried time and again to stop, but with no success. Without our even realizing it, we find ourselves falling right back into the very thing we want to avoid.

If you're having trouble getting rid of a bad habit, you're right where God can work with you. You recognize your weakness against the strength of an addiction, whether a seemingly harmless one or something interfering with your relationships, well-being, and enjoyment of life. Because you realize you can't go it alone, you're ready for God's help.

God is a habit-buster. Open yourself to His presence. Allow His great power to quash the bad and bring on the good–good thoughts, good desires, good decisions, good habits. Step by step, He will open the way for you. How? Perhaps through the prompting of His Spirit in you...through the encouragement of caring friends...through the helpful words of a trusted minister or counselor.

Two steps forward, one step back? That's okay. Celebrate the one step you've gone forward, and keep on stepping!

In all things, God works to your good and for your good.

Whatever is true, whatever is noble, whatever is right, whatever is pure, whatever is lovely, whatever is admirable—if anything is excellent or praiseworthy—think about such things.

PHILIPPIANS 4:8 NIV

Habit is either the best of servants or the worst of masters.

NATHANIEL EMMONS

It's easier to prevent bad habits than to break them.

PROVERB

Habit is habit, and not to be flung out of the window by any man, but coaxed downstairs a step at a time.

MARK TWAIN

As a single footstep will not make a path on the earth, so a single thought will not make a pathway in the mind. To make a deep physical path, we walk again and again. To make a deep mental path, we must think over and over the kind of thoughts we wish to dominate our lives.

Henry David Thoreau

Memories

God gave us memory that we might have roses in December.

James M. Barrie

Best Memories

Personal memories can work for us or against us. When they crush us with regret over what could have happened, should have happened, and might have happened, memories are our worst enemy. They keep us captured in a past no amount of regret can change.

But when we gain wisdom from the past… when we select memories that lift us up, inspire us, teach us, and motivate us…when we keep in mind and heart memories that remind us how blessed we have been, then our memories work for us. They're like good friends we can call on whenever we want to remind ourselves of the life lessons experience has brought us, or recall the pleasures, good times, and enjoyments of yesterday.

Memories of how God has come through for you in the past are the most helpful memories of all. They remind you of the many times He has protected you, lifted you out of dicey situations, given you exactly what you needed when you needed it, and sent the right person at just the right time. Pile up these memories, and you have a mountain of reasons to rely on Him today, tomorrow, and forever!

*Memory is the cabinet of imagination,
the treasury of reason, the registry of conscience,
and the council chamber of thought.*

Basil of Caesarea

*Make it a rule of life never to regret
and never to look back. Regret is an appalling
waste of energy; you can't build on it;
it's only good for wallowing in.*

Katherine Mansfield

*Reflect upon your present blessings,
of which every man has many—not on your past
misfortunes, of which all men have some.*

Charles Dickens

Life can only be understood backwards,
but it must be lived forwards.
SØREN KIERKEGAARD

Remember, O LORD, thy tender mercies and thy lovingkindnesses; for they have been ever of old.
PSALM 25:6

"Old times" never come back, and I suppose it's just as well. What comes back is a new morning every day in the year, and that's better.
GEORGE E. WOODBERRY

Resolve

Stand firm in the Lord.

Philippians 4:1 NIV

RESOLVE TO SUCCEED

Ask a hundred people to define success in life, and you're sure to hear a hundred different answers. Some will claim that success means possessing money, fame, power, or status; others will say it's having a solid marriage and raising happy, healthy children; still others will say success means personal fulfillment and peace of mind, regardless of outward circumstances.

Now it's your turn. What does success mean to you? Keep in mind that what's most important to you–what defines your success–might be quite different from what someone else expects of you or what the world tells you it ought to be. Tap into your deepest beliefs and values; think about where you would like to be ten or twenty years from now. Once your heart has spoken, resolve to succeed.

Determine what you need to do, and do a little each day. Perhaps you won't see progress immediately, but it will come in time. Maybe there are challenges to overcome now, or they might come later, but you have what it takes to surmount them. Most importantly, resolve to pray for lasting faith, because remaining close to God is the root of all true success at every stage of life.

Be like a postage stamp.
Stick to one thing until you get there.
JOSH BILLINGS

To tend, unfailingly, unflinchingly,
towards a goal, is the secret of success.
ANNA PAVLOVA

There must be a beginning of any great matter,
but the continuing unto the end until it be
thoroughly finished yields the true glory.
FRANCIS DRAKE

Fall seven times, stand up eight.
PROVERB

The block of granite which was an obstacle in the pathway of the weak becomes a stepping stone in the pathway of the strong.

THOMAS CARLYLE

Start by doing what's necessary, then what's possible, and suddenly you are doing the impossible.

FRANCIS OF ASSISI

If one advances confidently in the direction of his dreams, and endeavors to live the life which he has imagined, he will meet with success unexpected in common hours.

HENRY DAVID THOREAU

Direction

The way of progress is neither swift nor easy.

Marie Curie

READ THE DIRECTIONS

Don't you love it when product assembly and set-up are simple? The thing goes together easily, and intuition tells you where the battery fits and which buttons to push. Yet when intuition fails and you're besieged by a jumble of parts, pieces, cables, and cords, you're forced to do what you don't want to do: Read the directions.

When we enter a new stage of life, we might start out eagerly, thinking we know exactly what we want. When we're young, we're driven by energy and ambition; and when we're older, we believe we have the life experience to do things our own way. But what seemed so simple in the beginning turns more complicated. Besieged by an array of complex problems and unexpected hurdles, we wish we had read the directions before starting out.

If you're at that point now, give yourself two thumbs-up for courage, imagination, and spunk. You tried! But to make progress from here, you need to determine what's salvageable and what's not; what needs fixing, and who can help. It's a good time, too, to find where you are spiritually. When it comes to life's directions, God wrote the Book.

If you board the wrong train, it is no use running along the corridor in the other direction.

Dietrich Bonhoeffer

The strength of a man consists in finding out the way God is going and going that way.

Henry Ward Beecher

*Thy word is a lamp unto my feet,
and a light unto my path.*

Psalm 119:105

*Knowing is not enough, we must apply.
Willing is not enough, we must do.*

Johann Wolfgang von Goethe

The great thing in this world
is not so much where we stand,
as in what direction we are moving.
OLIVER WENDELL HOLMES

Even if you're on the right track,
you'll get run over if you just sit there.
WILL ROGERS

Pursue some path, however narrow and crooked,
in which you can walk with love and reverence.
HENRY DAVID THOREAU

Our deeds determine us,
as much as we determine our deeds.
GEORGE ELIOT

Hope

In his word do I hope.

Psalm 130:5

A Sure Hope

"I hope so." So often we say those words with a hang-dog frown and a pity-me sigh of resignation. We hope things work out (but we know they won't). We hope we get what we want (but probably not). Our hope is simply wishful thinking.

There's another kind of hope, and that's spiritual hope. When we risk placing our trust in God's promises of love, forgiveness, and life forever with Him, we're talking about spiritual hope. We use the word "hope" because we can't see or touch it, or even prove it scientifically. But unlike wishful thinking, Spirit-given hope has certainty attached. God has spoken! A woeful "I hope so" becomes a joyful and joy-filled "I know so!"

Your hope in and reliance on all God's promises swaps fear and uncertainty for security and optimism founded on trust in God. With hope firmly placed in Him, you're able to move forward in confidence, even if the way is unclear right now, and you're taking it one step at a time. With your heart and mind invigorated with spiritual hope, you can face the future knowing that things will work out for you. And that's more than wishful thinking–it's for sure!

Faith is a living, daring confidence in God's grace, so sure and certain that a man could stake his life on it a thousand times.

Martin Luther

"For I know the plans I have for you," declares the LORD, "plans to prosper you and not to harm you, plans to give you hope and a future."

Jeremiah 29:11 NIV

As long as matters are really hopeful,
hope is mere flattery or platitude;
it is only when everything is hopeless
that hope begins to be a strength.

G. K. Chesterton

The only limit to our realization of tomorrow will be our doubts of today. Let us move forward with strong and active faith.

FRANKLIN DELANO ROOSEVELT

How very little can be done under the spirit of fear.

FLORENCE NIGHTINGALE

When it is dark enough, you can see the stars.

RALPH WALDO EMERSON

Perspective

Be of good cheer.

John 16:33

PERSPECTIVE IS A CHOICE

Little bumps in the road swell into huge hurdles. Serious concerns morph into everything-that's-wrong-with-the-world issues. You've met that kind of person, haven't you? And no doubt you've met the opposite kind of person–aware, intelligent, and involved, yet upbeat and optimistic no matter what the day brings.

Perspective makes a big difference. Though we might find ourselves naturally more inclined to melancholy and pessimism over bubbly optimism, we don't have to accept, much less harbor, negative thoughts. God gave us the ability to choose our attitude. We can wake up in the morning and choose to approach the day as a burden or a discovery, a problem or an opportunity to kick up our high heels (or flip flops) and really live.

Worries, anxieties, and fear are huge obstacles to a positive spin on life, and God's Spirit works in you to remove those impediments. When you place your trust in Him and you know He'll be with you no matter what happens, there's nothing to stop you from welcoming the coming hours with optimism and enthusiasm.

Little bumps in the road or huge hurdles? Serious concerns or uncontrollable chaos? Your perspective is the most important choice you'll make today.

The world is a looking glass and gives back to every man the reflection of his own face. Frown at it and it will in turn look sourly upon you; laugh at it and with it, and it is a jolly, kind companion.

William Makepeace Thackeray

Could we change our attitude, we should not only see life differently, but life itself would come to be different. Life would undergo a change of appearance because we ourselves had undergone a change in attitude.

Katherine Mansfield

If I were to wish for anything, I should not wish for wealth and power, but for the passionate sense of the potential, for the eye which, ever young and ardent, sees the possible.

Søren Kierkegaard

I make the most of all that comes
and the least of all that goes.

SARA TEASDALE

The people who get on in this world
are the people who get up and look for the
circumstances they want, and if they
can't find them, make them.

GEORGE BERNARD SHAW

To be interested in the changing seasons
is a happier state of mind than to be
hopelessly in love with spring.

GEORGE SANTAYANA

Act, look, feel successful,
conduct yourself accordingly, and you will be
amazed at the positive results.

WILLIAM JAMES

Authenticity

Learn what you are, and be such.

Pindar

PATH TO AUTHENTICITY

As women today, we enjoy options only rarely available to our mothers and grandmothers. At every stage in life, we're less constrained than ever before by norms and expectations dictating what we can or should do. Yay!

But options get us into trouble when we grasp at too many of them. Either because we expect superhuman strength of ourselves or we think others expect it of us, we want everything! And when we can't manage all the roles we've taken on? We feel diminished, as if we somehow didn't measure up...as if we've failed.

Despite the glossy (and fictional) gals of TV dramas, you were never meant to do it all. God gave you specific gifts, and He invites you to use them in a coherent, manageable, and fulfilling way. He created you to be yourself, whether you choose to follow in the footsteps of women who walk ahead of you, or blaze new trails for women coming after you.

At this time in your life, opt for the path that lets you travel as a real, genuine, authentic, and beautiful woman–because that's the choice God has in mind for you.

No man, for any considerable period,
can wear one face to himself, and another to
the multitude, without finally getting
bewildered as to which may be the true.

Nathaniel Hawthorne

Not until we are lost do we begin
to understand ourselves.

Henry David Thoreau

To know what you prefer, instead of humbly
saying "Amen" to what the world tells you you
ought to prefer, is to have kept your soul alive.

Robert Louis Stevenson

There is a great deal of unmapped country
within us which would have to be taken
into account in an explanation
of our gusts and storms.

George Eliot

Our body is not made of iron. Our strength is not that of stone. Live and hope in the Lord, and let your service be according to reason.

CLARE OF ASSISI

Seek out that particular mental attribute which makes you feel most deeply and vitally alive, along with which comes the inner voice which says, "This is the real me," and when you have found that attitude, follow it.

WILLIAM JAMES

There are diversities of gifts, but the same Spirit.

1 CORINTHIANS 12:4

Giving

When I give,
I give myself.

Walt Whitman

Blessing of Giving

"Count your blessings!" we admonish ourselves when we start to complain. Yes, God has blessed us with all good things, starting with the gift of life and breath. How could anyone count them all?

Our immeasurable blessings reveal God as good, generous, practical, and compassionate as He serves our physical and spiritual needs. His giving to us provides a picture of what it's like to live a God-like life, and give more.

Throughout our lives, the years open ever more opportunities to give. Perhaps at one stage we give our time and skills to those who would be blessed by our help, while at another we're able to offer financial resources to those in need. Setbacks and adversities of the past equip us to comfort and encourage others experiencing similar trials. What we've learned so far can supply direction and guidance for anyone who comes to us with a question or problem.

God-like giving–generous giving–shares the blessings God has given you with your family, friends, community, and beyond. Attentive listening, thoughtful counsel, practical help, and heartfelt prayer are all ways you can follow His example. When you do, the blessing of genuine joy is yours.

No one is useless in this world
who lightens the burdens of another.
CHARLES DICKENS

Joy can be real only if people look upon their
life as a service, and have a definite object in life
outside themselves and their personal happiness.
LEO TOLSTOY

I have given you an example,
that ye should do as I have done to you.
JOHN 13:15

What do we live for if not to make the world less
difficult for each other?
GEORGE ELIOT

The very act of giving, with its apparent loss, tends to throw us upon Spirit and makes us depend upon God for supply.

Henry Thomas Hamblin

Do all the good you can, by all the means you can, in all the ways you can, in all the places you can, at all the times you can, to all the people you can, as long as you can.

John Wesley

Miss no single opportunity of making some small sacrifice, here by a smiling look, there by a kindly word; always doing the smallest right and doing it all for love.

Thérèse of Lisieux

Promise

The Lord is not slack concerning his promise.

2 Peter 3:9

God's Promise

Need a vacation? Most of us would say "Yes!" to the idea of going away somewhere and relaxing in the sunshine or swooshing down the ski slopes. The best vacations bring us back home renewed, refreshed, and ready to take on our regular routine.

One kind of vacation works the opposite way, and that's a spiritual vacation. Spiritual vacations, when we drift away from daily prayer and meditation...from faithfulness to God's will for our lives... from commitment to being the person He wants us to be...leave us spiritually depleted. We feel far from God because we have wandered away from the consciousness of His presence and the knowledge of His care. While we may have opened to Him easily and effortlessly in the past, now we're unsure how to even begin the heartfelt prayer we long to say.

Do you want to return "home" to your heavenly Father? Wherever a spiritual vacation has taken you and however long it has been, God welcomes you back with open arms. He is willing to forgive and eager to restore you to the family of His faithful people. He will renew you and refresh you, and spiritual vitality will return. That's not just a promise–it's His promise.

Whether we stumble, or whether we fall,
we must only think of rising again
and going on in our course.
François Fénelon

I am not a tentative person. Whatever I do,
I give up my whole self to it.
Edna St. Vincent Millay

Now I am steel-set: I follow the call to the clear
radiance and glow of the heights.
Henrik Ibsen

Faith is one of the forces by which men live,
and the total absence of it means collapse.
William James

You do not have to change God's will or make
God change His mind towards you,
but only to become changed yourself,
in order to be made at-one, or brought in tune,
with the good that God has prepared for you.

HENRY THOMAS HAMBLIN

Out of the chill and the shadow,
Into the thrill and the shine;
Out of the dearth and the famine,
Into the fulness divine.

MARGARET ELIZABETH SANGSTER

Spirituality

Seek those things which are above.

Colossians 3:1

THE SPIRITUAL LIFE

If we call ourselves "spiritual," we're right. God has given each one of us a visible body and an invisible soul. But consider all the attention we pay to the body! We feed it and dress it and exercise it. Some of us even spend embarrassing amounts of time (and money) coaxing it to look fifteen years younger!

Meanwhile, the soul cries "Unfair!" as it sits there wondering when we're ever going to get around to doing something for it. A meal, maybe? Souls get strong on soul food, such as the words of Scripture and the writings of wise and inspired teachers. Heavenly minded souls, dressed in love, joy, and peace, get great exercise in acts of goodness, kindness, and compassion. They stay fresh and vibrant in every stage in life when they're nurtured in spiritual thoughts, words, and actions.

If you've played favorites lately and your soul feels abandoned, start balancing things out. Ask God to make the needs of your invisible soul visible to your heart and mind. Rather than simply acknowledge you have a soul, use it to grow closer to God and build a lively and living relationship with Him. And since God is as present as your soul, it sounds like a perfect match!

If man is not made for God,
why is he happy only in God? If man is made
for God, why is he opposed to God?

Blaise Pascal

Let us remember that within us there is a palace
of immense magnificence.

Teresa of Avila

The majority of men live without being thoroughly conscious that they are spiritual beings.

Søren Kierkegaard

It is only with the heart that one can see rightly.
What is essential is invisible to the eye.

Antoine de Saint-Exupéry

We are not human beings having a spiritual experience. We are spiritual beings having a human experience.

Pierre Teilhard de Chardin

By confronting us with irreducible mysteries that stretch our daily vision to include infinity, nature opens an inviting and guiding path toward a spiritual life.

Thomas More

The spirit of man is an inward flame; a lamp the world blows upon but never puts out.

Margot Asquith

Angels

All God's angels
come to us disguised.

James Russell Lowell

Angels in Disguise

Think of angels, and a chorus of winged and haloed heavenly beings comes to mind. Though no one knows exactly what angels look like, we do know that they're real. Scripture tells us that angels are God's invisible messengers, created by

Him to watch over us and carry out His commands on Earth.

Just as real, but often taken for granted, are God's visible angels. We won't find them with feathered wings attached to their shoulder blades, but their heavenly ways sweeten our days and brighten our years. These are the "angels" who comfort us in grief and rejoice with us in celebration...encourage us when our confidence flags and lighten our load with their humor, advice, and friendship.

We might fail to recognize these God-sent angels because they come to us as family members, friends, coworkers, and sometimes even strangers. We may take them for granted because–well, they're always there for us, right? And that's the heavenly part of it!

You'll know your special angels not by any particular physical feature–they come in all shapes and sizes. Instead, you'll know them by the heavenly things they do and say every day.

Make yourself familiar with the angels,
and behold them frequently in spirit;
for, without being seen,
they are present with you.

FRANCIS DE SALES

He shall give his angels charge over thee,
to keep thee in all thy ways.

PSALM 91:11

Let us not be justices of the peace,
but angels of peace.

THÉRÈSE OF LISIEUX

An angel can illuminate the thought and mind of man by strengthening the power of vision.

Thomas Aquinas

We are each of us angels with only one wing, and we can only fly by embracing one another.

Lucretius

Be not forgetful to entertain strangers: for thereby some have entertained angels unawares.

Hebrews 13:2

The guardian angels of life sometimes fly so high as to be beyond our sight, but they are always looking down upon us.

Jean Paul Richter

Wisdom

Wisdom is the principal thing; therefore get wisdom.

Proverbs 4:7

Get Wisdom

So who's the wise guy? No, not the prankster, nor the comedian who responds to every comment with a sassy comeback–the comeback it takes the rest of us two hours to formulate. It's not even the person with an enviable range of knowledge. The real wise guys (and gals) are the ones who possess God-given wisdom.

God, whose wisdom goes beyond our imagining, willingly showers us with wisdom. All He asks us to do is request His wisdom, beginning with the admission that on our own, we lack heavenly smarts. We may be witty, clever, and wise in the ways of the world, or have gone to school and gained a vast store of knowledge about the world. But true wisdom? That's out of this world!

Yes, true wisdom comes from above. We receive it as we read Scripture, reflect on its message, and apply it to our daily life. We get it by observing how mature, godly people respond to their challenges, and by listening when those mature in faith counsel us. And most reassuring of all, we can expect wisdom when we ask God for it, because He has promised to generously give it.

Who's wise? Easy–you are!

If any of you lack wisdom, let him ask of God, that giveth to all men liberally.

James 1:5

The most manifest sign of wisdom is a continual cheerfulness: her state is like that of things in the regions above the moon, always clear and serene.

Michel de Montaigne

Make wisdom your provision for the journey from youth to old age, for it is a more certain support than all other possessions.

Diogenes

Wisdom outweighs any wealth.

Sophocles

To know that which before us lies
in daily life is the prime wisdom.
JOHN MILTON

Honesty is the first chapter
in the book of wisdom.
THOMAS JEFFERSON

Wisdom is not finally tested in schools;
Wisdom cannot be pass'd from one having it,
to another not having it;
Wisdom is of the soul, is not susceptible of proof,
is its own proof.
WALT WHITMAN

Believe

I gave in and admitted that God was God.

C.S. Lewis

GOTTA BELIEVE IT!

Some say they doubt the existence of God. They'd prefer to let His identity remain undetermined rather than take a stand on the matter. Yet doubting itself is a stand–and an unstable one.

Doubt leaves us vulnerable to cynicism, faulty reasoning, and bogus claims. It also may serve as an excuse not to grapple with life-changing questions, such as, "Who is God?" and "Am I accountable to Him?"

God-planted faith answers those questions. Faith assures us of His existence, beyond what we can perceive in the wonder and complexity of creation. It clarifies what we can discern in our ability to think, feel, sense, and reflect on the world around us. Faith, nurtured by God, opens our spiritual eyes to the fact of God, as well as His presence and power in our lives, and His love and compassion toward us.

An acknowledgement of God's existence is like the beginning of a voyage to an exotic land. You start out with an idea of where you're going, but when you get there, you discover more peace, purpose, satisfaction, and fulfillment than you ever thought possible. The first step? *Believe.*

It is the heart which experiences God,
and not the reason. This, then, is faith:
God felt by heart, not by the reason.
BLAISE PASCAL

Now faith is being sure of what we hope for and
certain of what we do not see.
HEBREWS 11:1 NIV

On the day I first really believed in God,
for the first time life made sense to me
and the world had meaning.
DAG HAMMARSKJÖLD

Faith is to believe, on the word of God,
what we do not see, and its reward is
to see and enjoy what we believe.
AUGUSTINE

What is the use of having faith?
It is to connect the soul with God.

HENRY DRUMMOND

The whole course of things goes to teach us faith.
We need only obey. There is guidance
for each of us, and by lowly listening
we shall hear the right word.

RALPH WALDO EMERSON

Faith is an excitement and an enthusiasm:
it is a condition of intellectual magnificence
to which we must cling as to a treasure,
and not squander on our way through life in
the small coin of empty words.

GEORGE SAND

Blessing

The LORD bless you and keep you.

Numbers 6:24 NIV

Heart of Blessing

Picture in your mind the faces of those you love. Because of the deep affection you hold in your heart, you desire only the best for them. You do everything you can to bless their lives. The love you feel for one does not diminish the love you feel for another–you love each with an intense and fervent love. The blessings you shower on one may be different from the blessings you shower on another, but all these blessings come from your loving heart.

Your love for those closest to you is only a small measure of the love God feels for you. From before you were born, He knew you and loved you, and the years have changed nothing. No matter where life has taken you, the strong bond of love from Him to you remains the same.

Today, God continues to shower you with blessings. Are they the same blessings He has given to someone else? Do they always look like what you might expect? Probably not! But all your blessings, including the privilege of life itself, emanate from one awesome heart of love–God's. All play into the fantastic plans God has in mind for you, now and forever.

God Bless You